Amazing Animal Babies

WRITTEN BY
CHRISTOPHER MAYNARD

DORLING KINDERSLEY
London · New York · Stuttgart

A Dorling Kindersley Book

Editor Bernadette Crowley
Art editor Hans Verkroost
Assistant editor David Fung
Managing editor Sophie Mitchell
Managing art editor Miranda Kennedy
Production Shelagh Gibson

Illustrations by Ruth Lindsay, Julie Anderson and John Hutchinson
Photography by Peter Downs (pp 8-9); Mike Dunning (pp 10-11, 20-21, 28-29);
Gary Higgins (pp 12-13); Jane Burton (pp 14-15, 18-19); Nick Parfitt (pp 16-17);
Oxford Scientific Films (pp 22-23); Peter Anderson (pp 24-25); Neil Fletcher (pp 27)
Animals supplied by The Chipperfield Organisation (pp 8-9);
Marwell Zoological Park (pp 10-11, 16-17, 28-29); Trevor Smith's Animal World (pp 20-21);
Windsor Safari Park (pp 24-25); Birdland (p 27)
Editorial consultant Caroline Brett

First published in Great Britain in 1993 by
Dorling Kindersley Limited,
9 Henrietta Street, London, WC2E 8PS

A CIP catalogue record for this book
is available from the British Library

ISBN 07513 5026 5

Colour reproduction by Colourscan, Singapore
Printed in Italy by A. Mondadori Editore, Verona

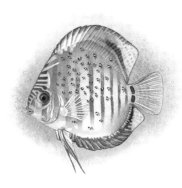

Contents

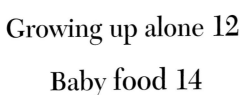

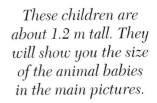

These children are about 1.2 m tall. They will show you the size of the animal babies in the main pictures.

New arrivals

Millions of baby animals are born every day. They may break their way out of an egg, or come out of their mother live, as humans do. From then on they must grow and learn how to survive in a world full of danger.

Helpless chick

A falcon chick is weak and naked when it hatches from its egg. After a few days the chick grows a thick coat of fluffy feathers, called down. The down keeps it warm as it waits for Mum and Dad to bring food back to the nest.

White beauty

Newborn baby tigers, called cubs, are born blind, helpless, and covered with striped fur. This white tiger cub is 12 weeks old and can run and play. It cannot kill its own food yet and needs to be fed by its parents.

White tigers are very rare

Quick start

A baby wildebeest is born headfirst. Within five minutes it can stand and trot. Wildebeests live in large groups and are always on the move. If a newborn baby did not get up quickly, it would be left behind.

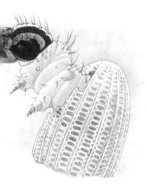

Breaking out

This caterpillar is hatching from its egg. A butterfly laid the egg on a leaf, which the caterpillar will eat. Most insects do not look after their young, but they always try to lay their eggs on or near something the young can eat when they hatch.

A ride on the back

Poison-arrow frogs lay their eggs on land. When the baby frogs, called tadpoles, hatch, they are carried to the water by one of their parents.

Baby care

Human babies need to be well cared for to survive. Human young are looked after by their parents for longer than any other animal.

Jaws

On their own

Baby insects, known as nymphs or larvae, usually have to fend for themselves. The larva of the antlion fly has big, strong jaws with which it kills ants and sucks out their juices.

All in the family

Animal families help to take care of baby animals in much the same way that human families care for their children. Animal or human, it's a really tough job at times.

Father

Danger mouth

Mouthbrooder fish babies stay close to Mum as she swims. If danger threatens, Mum opens her mouth wide and the babies dart inside to take cover.

Taking out the nappies

It's a tough job keeping a nest of young birds clean. Baby thrushes lay their droppings in a neat sac, or pouch. This makes life easier for the parents, who simply pick up the sacs and dump them elsewhere.

Are you my mother?

Ducklings leave the nest soon after hatching. They will follow the first large object they see, which is usually their mother. But should a human be walking past, they may trail after him or her!

Golden boy

This golden lion tamarin baby is clinging tightly to his mother's back while his father sits close by. Dad usually carries him, but Mum takes him to suckle (drink her milk) at mealtimes.

Wolf girls

In 1920 two young girls were found living with a pack of wolves in the Indian jungle. The wolves had raised them as if they were wolf cubs. The girls howled like wolves, could run only on all fours, and ate only meat.

Clean start

A zebra mother spends time licking her newborn baby. This not only cleans the baby, but helps the mother to get to know the look and smell of it. Then she can recognize it among other baby zebras.

Baby

Mother

Lunch bunch

In a pride, or group of lions, a lioness will suckle any cub which begs for milk. All the lionesses in the pride are related, so if the cub is not her own, it will be a niece, nephew, or cousin.

Growing up alone

Some egg-laying animals do not protect their eggs and never see their young. It isn't as cruel as it sounds. When the babies hatch, they are well able to look after themselves.

Eat up your egg
Common frogs lay thousands of eggs in a pond and then leave them. After hatching, the tadpoles feed on the yolk of their eggs for a while.

Hungry cuckoo chick

Eggs galore
Animals which do not look after their eggs usually lay plenty of them. The giant clam is the champion egg layer. It shoots out a cloud of one billion eggs once a year.

Crafty cuckoos
A mother cuckoo lays an egg in another bird's nest. The cuckoo chick usually hatches first, then shoves the other eggs out of the nest. This way it gets all the attention – and all the food – from its new mother.

Killer bees

Cuckoo bees lay their eggs in the nests of other bees. The cuckoo bee larvae hatch first and crush the other eggs. They then feast on the store of food which was meant for their victims.

A mallee fowl chick hatching in its underground nest

A handy snack

Ladybirds lay their eggs near small bugs called aphids (*ay-fids*), which live on plants. When the ladybird larvae hatch, they feast on the aphids.

Early flight

Most bird chicks cannot survive without their parents, but mallee fowl chicks are different. They are almost fully feathered when they break out of the egg, and they can fly the very next day.

 Pipit

The pipit thinks the cuckoo is her chick, even though it is twice her size

Baby navigators

European eels swim thousands of kilometres across the Atlantic Ocean to the Sargasso Sea to lay their eggs. Then they die. After hatching, the baby eels swim back across the Atlantic to the rivers where their parents grew up.

Baby food

Some baby animals are fed by their parents, such as babies who drink their mother's milk. Other babies have to find their own food. This means they often have to battle with, and kill, other living creatures.

Sticky kisses
For the first few weeks of their life, discus fish babies feed on a sticky liquid which comes out of their parents' skin.

Crickets are a favourite night-time snack

Gecko shedding its skin

Go-getting gecko
Baby leopard geckos hunt at night, searching for juicy insects to eat. Insects are fast movers, but gecko babies can move at lightning speed. The baby gecko sheds its skin several times as it grows and becomes an adult.

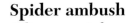

Spider ambush
A hungry pink-toed tarantula baby sometimes surprises a tasty insect by pouncing on it!

Stiff food
When mud wasp larvae hatch in their underground nest they have a meal of spiders waiting for them. The mother wasp catches spiders by injecting them with a poison, which paralyzes them. The spiders are still alive, but cannot move, when the larvae start eating them.

Nest full of spiders

Mud wasp larva feeding on the spiders

Fish soup
Albatross parents go on long feeding trips at sea. They return to the nest with a rich "soup" of fish and oil in their stomach, and bring the "soup" up for their hungry chick to gulp down.

Birds of a feather
Water-birds called grebes often pluck out a few of their feathers and feed them to their chicks.

Leopard geckos have sticky pads on their toes which allow them to climb up smooth surfaces

Ready, get set, grow!
An elephant seal pup drinks its mother's rich milk, which is packed with goodness. The milk helps the pup grow a layer of blubber, or fat, to keep out the cold.

15

In the nursery

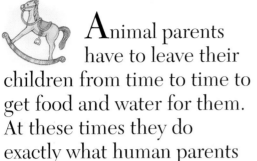

Animal parents have to leave their children from time to time to get food and water for them. At these times they do exactly what human parents do. They use baby-sitters.

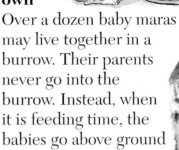

A room of their own
Over a dozen baby maras may live together in a burrow. Their parents never go into the burrow. Instead, when it is feeding time, the babies go above ground to join their parents.

These chicks will grow to be over 2 m tall

Taking turns
Meerkats live in groups where all members are related. The adults take it in turns to baby-sit the young meerkats while the other adults go hunting.

Ostriches are found in many parts of Africa

The chicks will lose their fluffy down and grow their adult feathers when they are about 1 year old

Caring crocs
Crocodile babies live in nurseries for the first few weeks of their life. This helps their mother to protect them from hungry enemies.

Go to your cell

Wasp larvae live in little cells until they become adults. Wasp nests have hundreds of six-sided cells, each containing one larva. When a larva hatches from its egg, it is fed pellets of chewed-up caterpillars and other insects.

Bat babies

When some bats go to feed, they leave their babies in nurseries. The babies are packed tightly so their little naked bodies stay warm.

Ostriches cannot fly, and are the largest birds

Male ostrich with group of chicks

Leader of the pack

Female ostriches let the male do the job of hatching their eggs. One male may end up with eggs from five females (up to 40 eggs in all). He can find himself leading a group containing dozens of youngsters.

Ostriches have strong legs for running fast

Water babies

A wide variety of babies live in seas, rivers, and ponds. Many live completely underwater. Other water babies spend their time splashing around on top of the water and diving for food.

Little terrors

Dragonfly nymphs live underwater in ponds and streams. They are fierce little hunters who will eat anything they can catch: worms, insects, tadpoles, and even small fish.

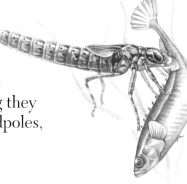

Men at work

When seahorses mate, the female squirts her eggs into a pouch in the male's belly. The male keeps the eggs until it is time for the babies to hatch. Then hundreds of tiny seahorses pop out.

A little help

River otter mothers give their babies swimming lessons. At a pup's very first swim, it may be so nervous of the water that it has to be pushed in!

Copycats

Baby mallard ducks can swim soon after they hatch, but they cannot fly for several weeks. They stay close to their mother for safety in case a hungry enemy should fancy them for dinner.

Going up for air

As soon as a baby blue whale is born its mother guides it to the water's surface for its first breath of air. Whales need to breathe air to live. They breathe through a hole on the top of their head, called a blowhole.

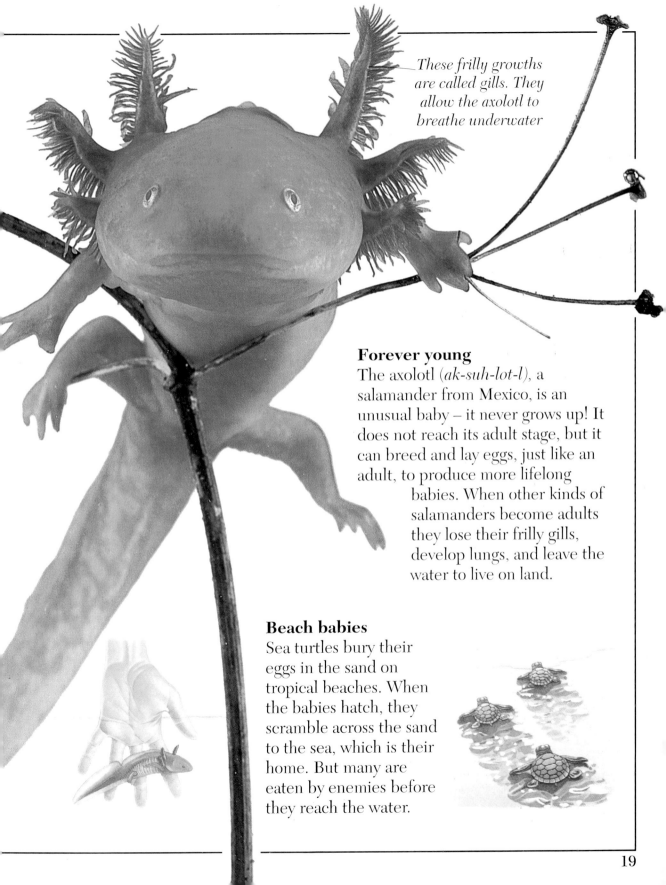

These frilly growths are called gills. They allow the axolotl to breathe underwater

Forever young

The axolotl (*ak-suh-lot-l*), a salamander from Mexico, is an unusual baby – it never grows up! It does not reach its adult stage, but it can breed and lay eggs, just like an adult, to produce more lifelong babies. When other kinds of salamanders become adults they lose their frilly gills, develop lungs, and leave the water to live on land.

Beach babies

Sea turtles bury their eggs in the sand on tropical beaches. When the babies hatch, they scramble across the sand to the sea, which is their home. But many are eaten by enemies before they reach the water.

Playschool

Young mammals spend lots of time playing. Play builds up muscles, develops fighting skills, and helps prepare young animals for adult life.

Rough house
Young animals are not the only ones who like to play. Parents sometimes get in on the act, too. The parents stay very calm, even when play gets rough. If they didn't, they might hurt their own babies.

Fishing school
Grizzly bear cubs watch closely as their mother catches salmon from a river. The cubs learn not only what is good to eat but also how to catch it.

These American black bear cubs are four months old

Learning to kill

From time to time, cheetah parents bring their cubs live prey so the cubs can practise killing skills.

Hard lessons

A baby hippo must learn to stay very close to Mum so it can be protected from danger. Every time the baby starts to wander off, Mum butts it with her large muzzle until it learns its lesson.

Having fun

Young chimps use the forest like a giant adventure playground as they swing through branches and climb up trunks and vines.

Play havoc

American black bear cubs spend much of their early days play-fighting and lying in the sun. Sometimes their play-fighting gets a bit rough, and Mum has to step in to calm the cubs down.

Fine feathered friends

Very few baby birds play, except for crows and ravens, which are among the most intelligent birds. Young ravens love to chase each other backwards and forwards in mock battles.

Baby transport

Some parents will pick up and carry their babies only when there is danger. Others are in the habit of carrying their babies whenever they want a ride.

Taken under the wing

If an African jacana chick is in any danger, its father will pick it up, tuck it under his wing, and run to safety.

Don't bite me

A baby raccoon is not hurt when its mother picks it up with her teeth. She grasps the back of the baby's neck where the skin is loose.

Claw

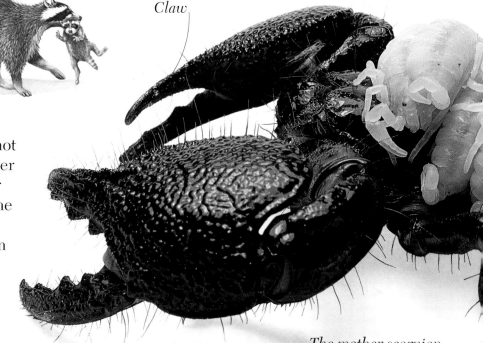

The mother scorpion will use her strong claws and fierce sting to defend her babies

Shrewd move

When a mother white-toothed shrew goes looking for food, her babies go too. Each baby uses its teeth to grip a tuft of hair on the baby ahead of it, forming a line. This "caravan" keeps the family together and helps protect the babies from enemies.

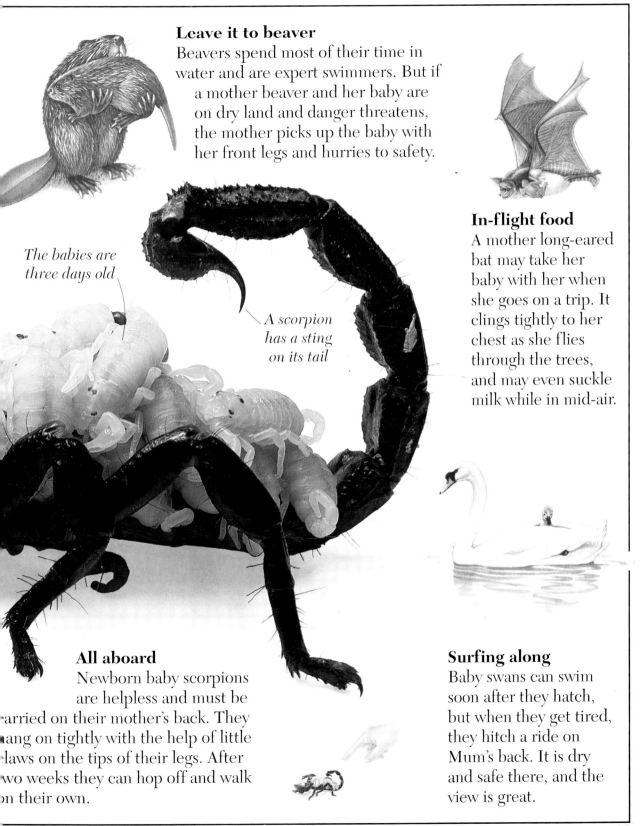

Leave it to beaver

Beavers spend most of their time in water and are expert swimmers. But if a mother beaver and her baby are on dry land and danger threatens, the mother picks up the baby with her front legs and hurries to safety.

The babies are three days old

A scorpion has a sting on its tail

In-flight food

A mother long-eared bat may take her baby with her when she goes on a trip. It clings tightly to her chest as she flies through the trees, and may even suckle milk while in mid-air.

All aboard

Newborn baby scorpions are helpless and must be carried on their mother's back. They hang on tightly with the help of little claws on the tips of their legs. After two weeks they can hop off and walk on their own.

Surfing along

Baby swans can swim soon after they hatch, but when they get tired, they hitch a ride on Mum's back. It is dry and safe there, and the view is great.

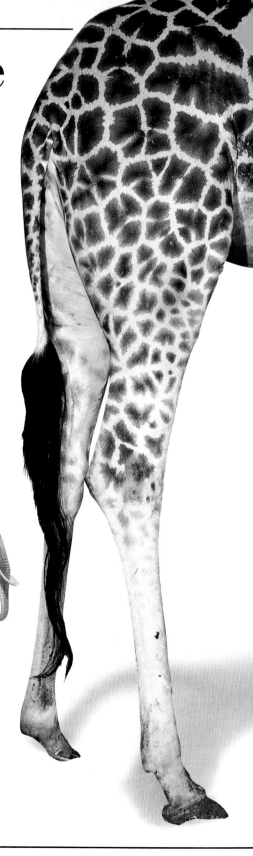

Little & large

Some newborn baby animals are so small they could slip through your fingers. But you would have a problem if you tried to cradle the biggest baby in your arms!

Tiny tot

An adult giant panda can weigh as much as a big adult human, but a newborn panda cub weighs only about 120 grams – that's less than the weight of a lemon.

Mighty mite

Baby elephants spend up to two years growing inside their mother – that's longer than any other animal. They are big babies when born, weighing about the same as four of your friends.

A cod fry in its egg

Eggs galore

A large Atlantic cod may lay up to six million eggs at one time. Each egg is see-through and tiny – no bigger than a pinhead. When the fry, or baby fish, hatch, they are about the size of your little fingernail.

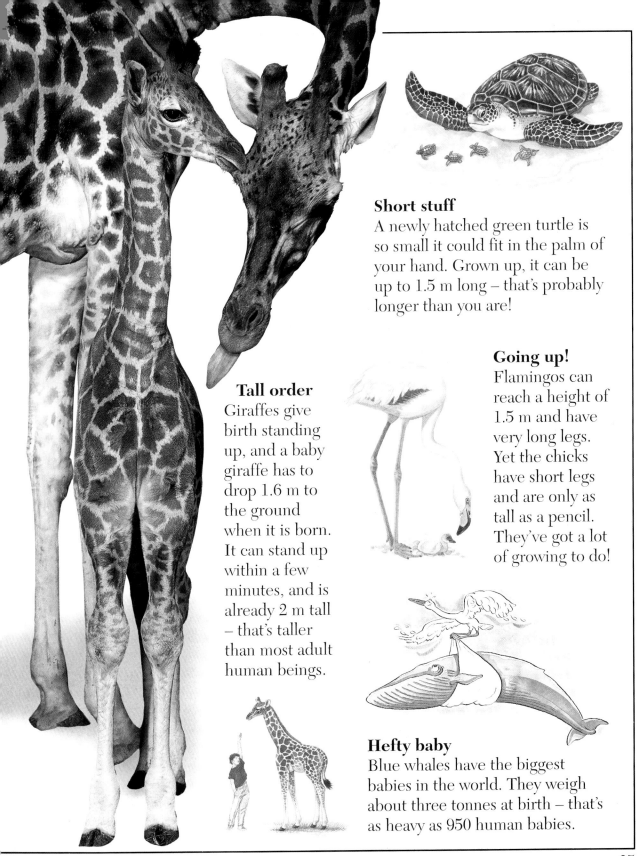

Short stuff
A newly hatched green turtle is so small it could fit in the palm of your hand. Grown up, it can be up to 1.5 m long – that's probably longer than you are!

Going up!
Flamingos can reach a height of 1.5 m and have very long legs. Yet the chicks have short legs and are only as tall as a pencil. They've got a lot of growing to do!

Tall order
Giraffes give birth standing up, and a baby giraffe has to drop 1.6 m to the ground when it is born. It can stand up within a few minutes, and is already 2 m tall – that's taller than most adult human beings.

Hefty baby
Blue whales have the biggest babies in the world. They weigh about three tonnes at birth – that's as heavy as 950 human babies.

Baby clothes

Newborn hedgehog

Spines shou a few hours later

Baby animals often look different from their parents. In most cases, this helps babies blend in with their surroundings, and makes them hard for hungry hunters to spot.

Spineless baby
A baby hedgehog is born with its first coat of spines lying flat under its skin. Within a few hours the spines pop up. An adult hedgehog has about 5,000 prickly spines in all.

White as snow
Harp seals live in the Arctic, where there is snow all year round. Newborn harp seals have a coat of thick white fur which makes them hard to see against the snow.

Stripes
European wild piglets have a brown coat with white stripes. This coat helps them blend in with the open woodlands where they wander with their big, dark-coloured mother.

Rainbow snakes
The colour of adult green pythons is, of course, green! Green python babies are usually yellow, but they can be blue, red, orange, and black.

Tufty chick   *Elegant parent*

Changing suits
A king penguin chick starts to lose its baby down when it is eight months old. It looks odd as tufts of down fall off to reveal the adult feathers underneath. Soon it will look as sleek and elegant as its parents.

Adult

Baby

Emperor's new clothes

Young emperor butterfly fish are dark blue with light blue and white circles. Adults have brilliant yellow and blue stripes. The young look different from the adults to show they are not rivals for food or living space. That is why adults let the young feed alongside them.

King penguins live in the Antarctic, where it is very cold. Thick down helps keep the chicks warm

Fluffy ball

King penguin chicks are covered with a thick brown down that makes them look like big balls of fluff. They are unable to go into the water until they grow their adult waterproof feathers.

Pocket babies

M arsupials are animals with a pouch in which they carry their babies. The babies stay in the pouch until they grow too big to fit in any more.

Piggyback baby

A baby koala leaves its mother's pouch when it grows too big to fit in. It then rides around on her back until it learns to fend for itself.

Leaving home

A baby kangaroo, called a joey, climbs into its mother's pouch headfirst, then curls itself around so its head pokes out.

A rough ride

An opossum gives birth to about 10 babies, which all live in her pouch – at first. After a while they grow too big to fit in. Then they move onto her back, and hang on for their lives!

Diving baby

The yapok has a waterproof pouch. This stops its babies drowning when it dives underwater for food.

Mini marsupials

A newborn joey is only the size of a jelly bean. It crawls into its mother's pouch and finds a teat from which it drinks its mother's milk.

Nice and snug

This wallaby has her joey safely tucked inside her pouch. After six months the joey will start taking short trips outside the pouch. But it will quickly leap in again at the first sign of danger.

It is warm and safe inside the pouch, and the view's good, too

Index